UTAH

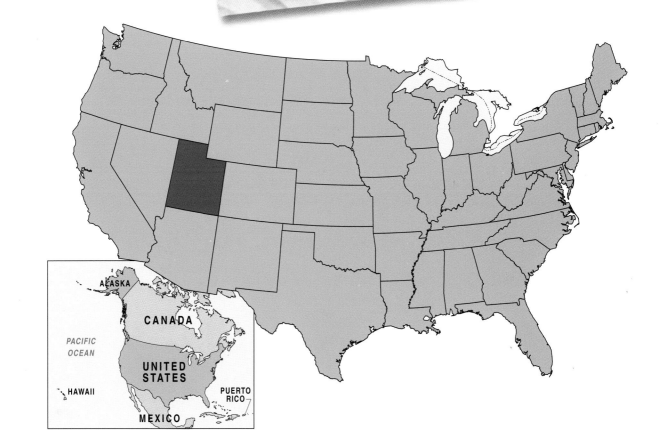

UTAH

HELLO
U.S.A.

by Karen Sirvaitis

Lerner Publications Company

You'll find this picture of a honeycomb at the beginning of each chapter in this book. Bees make honeycombs inside beehives. A beehive appears on Utah's state seal. Utah's state motto, Industry, is also related to the beehive. Like a beehive, Utah is a busy place with hardworking residents.

Cover (left): Rock formations called hoodoos, in Bryce Canyon National Park. Cover (right): Downhill skier near Salt Lake City. Pages 2–3: Downtown Salt Lake City and Wasatch Mountains. Page 3: Joshua tree, Beaver Dam Mountains, southwest Utah.

This book is available in two editions:
Library binding by Lerner Publications Company, a division of Lerner Publishing Group
Soft cover by First Avenue Editions, an imprint of Lerner Publishing Group
241 First Avenue North
Minneapolis, MN 55401 U.S.A.

Website address: www.lernerbooks.com

Library of Congress Cataloging-in-Publication Data

Sirvaitis, Karen, 1961–
    Utah / by Karen Sirvaitis — (Rev. and expanded 2nd ed.)
       p.   cm. — (Hello U.S.A.)
    Includes index.
    ISBN: 0–8225–4088–6 (lib. bdg. : alk. paper)
    ISBN: 0–8225–0796–X (pbk. : alk. paper)
    1. Utah—Juvenile literature. [1. Utah.] I. Title. II. Series.
F826.3 .S58 2002
979.2—dc21   2001006049

Manufactured in the United States of America
1 2 3 4 5 6 – JR – 07 06 05 04 03 02

CONTENTS

Bryce Canyon, in southern Utah, is famous for its rugged beauty.

THE LAND

A Varied Landscape

alty lakes, goblin-shaped rocks, dinosaur graveyards. Many Utahns would say a varied landscape is part of what makes their state unique. Snowcapped mountain peaks overlook miles of **desert** in one place, while a mighty river, a deep **canyon,** or a fertile valley can be found close by. Three land regions—the Great Basin, the Rocky Mountains, and the Colorado Plateau—define Utah.

The Great Basin region covers western Utah from north to south. Although it is a desert and one of the driest areas of the nation, the Great Basin includes Utah's largest body of water, Great Salt Lake. Its water is unusual because it is very salty—saltier than any of the oceans. For this reason, the lake is called an **inland sea.**

Utah's state flower is the sego lily.

7

N
W   E
S

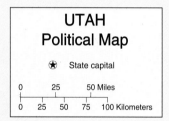

UTAH
Political Map

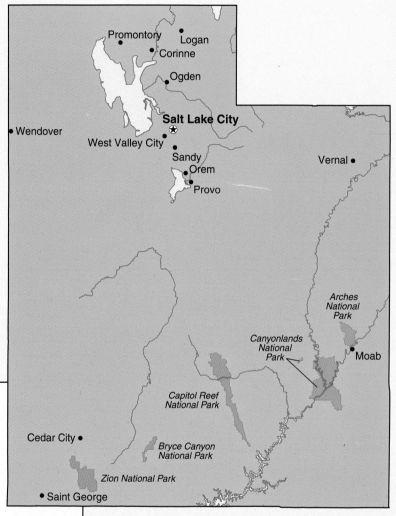

Promontory   • Logan

Corinne

• Ogden

Salt Lake City
⭐

• Wendover

West Valley City

Sandy

Orem

Provo

Vernal •

Arches
National
Park

Canyonlands
National
Park

• Moab

Capitol Reef
National Park

Bryce Canyon
National Park

Cedar City •

Zion National Park

• Saint George

The drawing of Utah on this page is called a political map. It shows features created by people, including cities, railways, and parks. The map on the facing page is called a physical map. It shows physical features of Utah, such as islands, mountains, rivers, and lakes. The colors represent a range of elevations, or heights above sea level (see legend box). This map also shows the geographical regions of Utah.

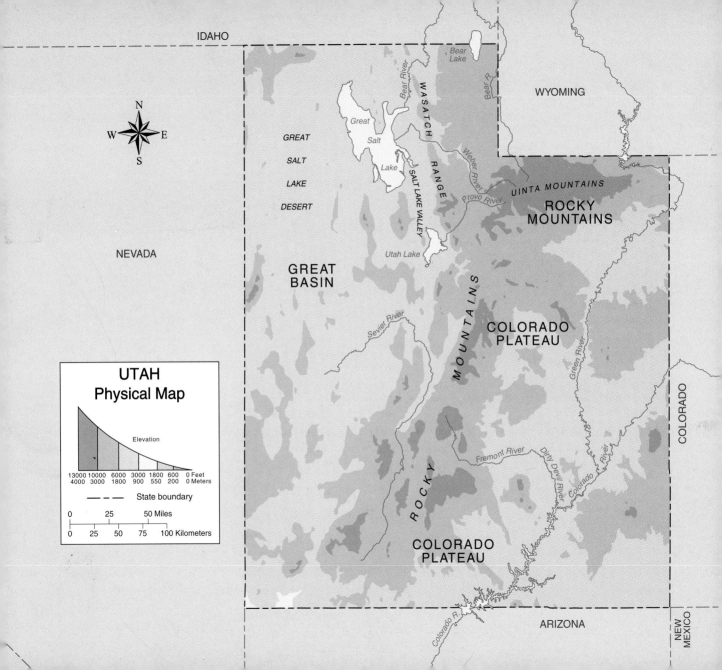

IDAHO

WYOMING

Bear Lake

Bear River

WASATCH RANGE

Bear R.

GREAT
SALT
LAKE
DESERT

Great
Salt
Lake

NEVADA

Weber River

Provo River

UINTA MOUNTAINS

ROCKY
MOUNTAINS

SALT LAKE VALLEY

GREAT
BASIN

Utah Lake

M O U N T A I N S

COLORADO
PLATEAU

Sevier River

Green River

COLORADO

ROCKY

Fremont River

Dirty Devil River

Colorado River

COLORADO
PLATEAU

UTAH
Physical Map

Elevation

| 13000 | 10000 | 6000 | 3000 | 1800 | 600 | 0 Feet |
| 4000 | 3000 | 1800 | 900 | 550 | 200 | 0 Meters |

– – – State boundary

0   25   50 Miles

0   25   50   75   100 Kilometers

Colorado R.

ARIZONA

NEW MEXICO

At Dinosaur National Monument in northeastern Utah, sandstone walls contain thousands of dinosaur fossils.

Spanning 1,700 square miles, Great Salt Lake is what remains of a much larger ancient lake that scientists call Bonneville. Thousands of years ago, Lake Bonneville covered much of the Great Basin. Over time, most of the water dried up, leaving Great Salt Lake and a broad stretch of **salt flats** that are packed as hard as concrete.

Another special feature of the state is the Uinta Range in the Rocky Mountain region of northeastern Utah. The Rockies, a nickname for the Rocky Mountains, span parts of the western United States and Canada. Of all the ranges included in this chain of mountains, only the Uinta extends west to east. Other ranges of the Rockies, including the Wasatch in Utah, run north to south.

The Colorado Plateau stretches across most of southern and eastern Utah. The **plateau,** a broad expanse of high land, is hard and rocky. Rivers have carved deep canyons in this region, most of which is too rugged for growing crops. Over millions of years, wind and rain have sculpted rocks on the plateau into strange shapes. Some of the rock formations look like castles, ships, or goblins.

Snow covers the peaks of the Wasatch Range during the winter months.

The Colorado River flows through the Colorado Plateau. The Colorado and its main **tributary,** the Green River, are major sources of waterpower for Utah. The Bear, Provo, and Weber Rivers begin in the Uinta Range. The Bear and Weber eventually drain into Great Salt Lake. The Provo empties into Utah

The Colorado River winds through Dead Horse Point State Park in eastern Utah.

Utah's desert areas receive very little rainfall.

Lake. The Sevier River is the longest waterway in southwestern Utah. Together these six rivers provide Utah with much of the water it needs for its farmlands, businesses, and households.

Even though it has many rivers, Utah is the second driest state in the country. (Nevada is the first.) Utah's deserts receive only about 5 inches of rain and snow each year, while the Rockies get up to 50 inches. Summertime temperatures in the desert can soar above 100° F. During the winter, temperatures in the mountains often drop below freezing.

Mormon pioneers gave the Joshua tree its name. The tree, which is a kind of yucca plant, can grow up to 25 feet tall.

A variety of plants and animals live in Utah. Some like the dry desert heat, while others need the coolness of high mountain areas. Most trees, such as blue spruce, white balsam, and aspen, grow on and around the mountains. These trees cannot survive on the scarce water available in the desert sands.

Cacti, sword plants, and sagebrush grow in the dry, rocky areas of the state. Southwestern Utah is home to the Joshua tree. This yucca is a tall, thick plant with white blossoms and some features of a tree. The Joshua tree got its name in the 1880s. Pioneers thought its limbs looked like arms lifted in prayer and called it Joshua, after a religious leader in the Bible.

Prairie dogs, bighorn sheep, bison (buffalo), mountain lions, coyotes, foxes, and beavers are among the many mammals that live in the state. Rattlesnakes are the only poisonous snakes found in Utah. Other reptiles include the desert tortoise and the Gila monster, the only poisonous lizard in the state.

Land turtles creep through Utah's deserts *(left)*. Coyotes make their homes in Utah's wilderness *(above)*.

People first began to explore Utah's vast landscape about 12,000 years ago.

THE HISTORY

Natives and Newcomers

Long before the United States existed, many groups of people lived throughout the North American continent. As long as 12,000 years ago, people first arrived in the area that later became Utah. Small groups of these Native Americans, or Indians, roamed the area. For food, they hunted animals and gathered wild berries, roots, and nuts.

Over time the Indians began to grow their food. They planted corn and beans. They also continued to hunt. These early Indians are called the Basketmakers because they crafted baskets, ropes, and sandals from dried grasses. The Basketmakers also made nets for catching small animals.

Cactus seeds, fruits, and stems were probably part of the Basketmakers' diet.

Eventually the Basketmakers channeled water from rivers to their fields. This practice is known as **irrigation.** The crops produced plenty of food for them.

As their farming practices developed, the Indians no longer moved from place to place to find their meals. Around A.D. 750, the Basketmakers began to build groups of permanent houses that were later

In Utah and throughout the southwestern United States, Pueblo Indians built their dwellings in cliffs. Some of the homes still exist.

Utah's Newspaper Rock State Park features rock carvings made by Native Americans.

called **pueblos,** the Spanish word for "villages." Those who built these villages eventually became known as Pueblo Indians.

To protect themselves from enemies, the Pueblos later built homes on cliffside ledges. But cliff dwellings could not protect the Indians completely. By 1300 the Pueblo Indians had disappeared from Utah, possibly due to attacks from more warlike groups.

Tribes that spoke Shoshonean languages had entered the area by the time the Pueblos had disappeared. These groups—the Ute, the Paiutes, the Gosiutes, and the Shoshones—shared certain customs, but each had its own form of government. They moved from place to place, hunting deer and antelope and gathering plants. For centuries the lifestyles of the Shoshonean-speaking peoples changed very little.

In 1776 two Spanish priests from Mexico, Francisco Atanasio Domínguez and Silvestre Vélez de Escalante, traveled through the Utah area. After the priests' exploration, Spain claimed Utah and opened up the region for white settlers.

Paiute villages were often raided by the Ute during the 1700s and early 1800s. The Ute took captives to sell to other Indian groups as slaves.

Spain did not send many people to live in the newly claimed land and had very little contact with the Indians. People from other countries, however, began to take an interest in the Spanish territory. Throughout the early 1800s, fur trappers and explorers came to Utah from many different places. These people rarely crossed paths with the Indians.

In 1776 an Indian guide led Escalante *(standing)* through what later became Utah.

Mormons passed the Uinta Range on their journey to Salt Lake Valley.

In 1846 a group of people from Nauvoo, Illinois, began looking westward for a new home. Their decision to move to Utah would eventually have a major impact on the lives of the Indians.

At Nauvoo stood the Church of Jesus Christ of Latter-day Saints. The church's members, called Latter-day Saints, or Mormons, studied the Bible along with some of their own religious works. The church urged members to help each other and to work hard. In just a few years, the Mormons had established a large community in Nauvoo and had helped to make the city one of the wealthiest in Illinois.

Mormons were often treated unfairly because of their success and because they held some uncommon beliefs. One such belief was that a man could practice **polygamy**—that is, he could have more than one wife at a time. Fearing they might be in danger, the Mormons fled Nauvoo shortly after their church's founder, Joseph Smith, was killed by an angry mob of non-Mormons in 1844.

Because Mormon men could marry several wives, Mormon families could become very large. This photograph shows several generations of one family.

Brigham Young

Brigham Young became the church's leader after Smith. Young planned to take the Latter-day Saints to a place where they could follow their religion in peace. Late in 1846, about 150 Mormons led by Brigham Young headed west. In 1847 they arrived in Salt Lake Valley, near the site that would become Salt Lake City. The valley was dry and appeared to be uninhabited.

Ute Indians lived close to where the Mormons chose to settle. The Ute distrusted the newcomers at first, but soon the two groups lived peacefully. The Indians taught the settlers which plants were safe to eat. Later, the Mormons gave the Indians food and clothing and preached the Mormon religion to some of them.

Mormon Pioneers

Brigham Young and the Mormon pioneers he led arrived in Salt Lake Valley on July 24, 1847. In the years that followed, thousands of Mormons from all over the world flocked to the valley. Most traveled in covered wagons, which were hard to control in the steep canyons. Those without wagons walked, pushing carts loaded with their belongings.

In 1847 Salt Lake Valley belonged to Mexico, which had won its independence from Spain in 1821. At the end of the Mexican-American War (1846–1848), Mexico lost much of its northern territory—including the Mormons' new home—to the United States.

Meanwhile, the Mormons were planting crops in the best soils of Salt Lake Valley. Together they built homes, schools, and churches. They irrigated their

Until crops could be harvested, Mormon pioneers relied on Ute Indians to help them find food.

crops with water from nearby rivers. By 1849 the Mormons had set up a government. They fixed boundaries for what they called the State of Deseret and chose Brigham Young as their governor.

The Mormons wanted Deseret to be admitted to the Union as the next state. Instead, the U.S. government in 1850 made Deseret into the Territory of Utah (named after the Ute Indians). As a territory, Utah had fewer rights than states did. But the U.S. government had decided that until Mormon men stopped taking several wives, Utah would remain a territory.

In 1849 someone in California hollered "Gold!" and the California gold rush began. For three years, thousands of miners stopped in Utah on their way to and from California. Tired, hungry, and sometimes rich, they were willing to pay the Mormons for food and fresh horses.

When business was good, some Mormons made a lot of money. Because Mormon church officials expected their followers to donate a **tithe** (10 percent of their income) to the church, the church was also getting rich.

The church often sent its members to other parts of the world to preach the Mormon gospel and to return with new believers. By 1852 more than 20,000 Mormons from all over the world had come to Utah. More and more, they settled in areas of Utah outside Salt Lake Valley.

Gold miners traveled through Utah on their way to California from 1849 to 1852.

The Indians were getting angry. The Mormons who were moving into other parts of the territory planted crops where wild berries had been growing. These Mormons built homes near streams and rivers where the Indians fished.

A Ute chief named Wakara, but known as Walker by settlers, decided to take action. In 1853 Chief Wakara led the Indians against the white settlers in what became known as the Walker War. By the end of the war in 1854, the Ute had not won back any territory, and the Mormons continued to build settlements.

A few years after the Walker War, another war broke out in Utah. This time the fighting was between the Mormon church and the

Chief Wakara led the Ute Indians in a war against Mormon settlers.

United States. The U.S. government had sent non-Mormon leaders to help govern the territory. These officials accused Mormons of ignoring the non-Mormon government. They said the Mormons turned to church officials for leadership.

The U.S. government sent troops to Utah in 1857, beginning the Utah War (also called the Mormon War). Soon after the troops reached Utah, the Mormons agreed to let a non-Mormon govern the territory. The army stayed to discourage trouble.

The soldiers left Utah in 1861 to fight in the Civil War, the war between the Northern and Southern states. Utah's government gathered a volunteer army to watch the Mormons and to keep the Ute from taking back any land from settlers. The leader of this army, Patrick Conner, often led attacks against the Indians.

Mountain Meadows Massacre

On September 11, 1857, a party of 140 non-Mormon pioneers was camped in a meadow just 40 miles outside of Cedar City in southern Utah. Having traveled hundreds of miles from Arkansas and Missouri, the men, women, and children were weary. The pioneers had had many troubles along their journey. Food was scarce, and the sun was blistering. The travelers probably felt that their problems could not get much worse.

Quite unexpectedly, a group of Mormon militiamen and some of their Indian friends attacked the wagon train, killing all but a few children. The Mormons claimed that the travelers had been responsible for the death of Joseph Smith, founder of the Mormon religion. The attack became known as the Mountain Meadows Massacre. After investigations, only one person—an Indian farmer—was executed for the crime.

Patrick Conner worked to force
Utah's Indians off their land.

Patrick Conner disliked the Mormons as
much as he disliked the Indians. He wanted
more non-Mormons to live in Utah. He had his
soldiers search for gold, silver, and iron—any metal
that would encourage non-Mormons to move to
Utah. Hundreds of non-Mormon miners arrived.
Some of them built the town of Corinne, the first
white, non-Mormon city in Utah.

Miners who wanted to dig on Indian lands ended
up battling Indians. To stop the fighting, the U.S.
government and Conner's troops pressured the
Indians into giving up their land. The U.S. government set aside areas of land, called **reservations,**
onto which the Indians of Utah were forced to move.

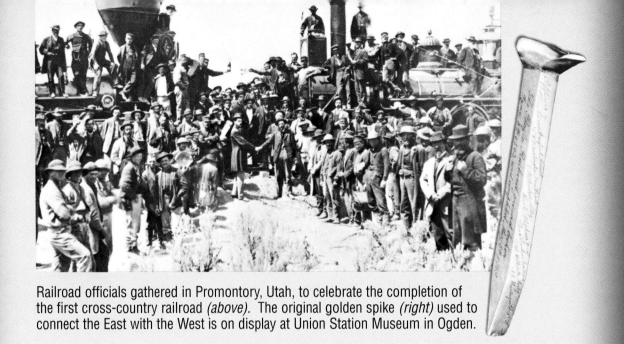

Railroad officials gathered in Promontory, Utah, to celebrate the completion of the first cross-country railroad *(above)*. The original golden spike *(right)* used to connect the East with the West is on display at Union Station Museum in Ogden.

The Golden Link

American businessmen first started planning a cross-country railroad in the 1850s. The two main companies involved were the Central Pacific Railroad and the Union Pacific Railroad. The Central Pacific started building toward the east from Sacramento, California, in 1863. The same year, the Union Pacific started building toward the west from Omaha, Nebraska.

On May 10, 1869, the two railroad lines met in Utah. The last link in America's first cross-country railroad was hammered into place in the town of Promontory. This feat meant that the Atlantic and Pacific coasts of the United States were finally connected. Trains soon carried people and goods across the country faster than horses or oxen could, and travel between the two coasts increased. Railroad companies began building more tracks throughout Utah and other states.

In the late 1800s, many immigrants came to Utah to work in the state's coal mines.

By the 1870s, the mining business in Utah was booming. Because the Mormon church at first discouraged its followers from working in the mines, mine owners asked people from places as far away as Greece, Finland, and Japan to work for their companies. **Immigrants** (newcomers from other countries), attracted by the jobs, came by the thousands. Utah's non-Mormon population grew rapidly.

Many of the territory's residents were eager to make Utah a state. But the Mormons' practice of polygamy was still a roadblock. In 1890 Mormon church officials agreed to not let a man have more than one wife, and in 1896 Utah became the 45th state in the Union.

Reed Smoot served as one
of Utah's first senators.

As a state, Utah could send politicians
to the nation's capital to vote on issues
concerning the whole country. In 1902
Utahns elected Reed Smoot as a
senator. Smoot's jobs involved working
as a lawmaker and attending meetings
of Congress.

Smoot was a Mormon, and U.S. government officials distrusted Mormons.
Politicians believed Mormons were still
practicing polygamy and that church
leaders had too much say in Utah's government.
Congress placed Smoot on trial, questioning
him about his duties in the church. After several
years in court, Congress had not cleared up all its

concerns about Smoot but decided to allow him to represent Utah as a senator. He did so for 30 years.

Other conflicts had good effects on Utah's economy during the first half of the 1900s. Mines in Utah furnished metals needed to make bullets and parts for planes, tanks, and guns used in World War I (1914–1918) and World War II (1939–1945). These items earned a lot of money for the state.

Utah workers made equipment for the U.S. military during World War II.

Since the late 1950s, Utah has been a testing ground for rockets.

Utah continued to make military equipment after the two world wars. The state has factories and test sites for rockets. These military sites are located on barren land, in areas where few people live.

During the 1960s, Utah educators wanted more money from the government for schools. When the government refused to give them the money, teachers in Utah and all over the United States protested. In 1965 the government gave the schools the money they needed.

Since the 1960s, workers have been building dams on Utah's rivers. The dams supply more water to the state's growing urban areas. Changes like these are not always good for the land. But Utahns have been careful to preserve much of Utah's beauty. In the 1980s, the state's tourist industry grew.

Outdoor adventurers flocked to Utah's many ski areas and five national parks. The state's computer software industry expanded during the 1980s and 1990s.

In 1995 Salt Lake City won the honor of hosting the 2002 Olympic Winter Games. The city spent millions of dollars preparing to welcome the world to Utah.

Salt Lake City built the Olympic Village to house athletes during the 2002 Olympic Winter Games.

Salt Lake City is Utah's biggest city and its state capital.

PEOPLE & ECONOMY

A Growing Population

 any Utahns live and work in or near Salt Lake Valley, where Brigham Young first led the Mormons. Utah's population reached just over 2.2 million in 2000. The state's large cities include Salt Lake City (the capital), Provo, Ogden, and Orem. More than 85 percent of the state's population lives in northern Utah because most other parts of the state are so dry and rugged.

Almost everyone living in Utah was born in the United States. Most of Utah's recent immigrants have come from Germany, Canada, Great Britain, or Mexico.

A small number of Utahns farm the state's rural areas.

Utah's Navajo Indians are descendants of some of the first people to live in the state.

African Americans, some of whom are descended from slaves brought by the first Mormons, make up less than 1 percent of Utah's population. Native Americans, who once were the only people in Utah, now number less than 2 percent. Most of the Ute live on the Uintah and Ouray Reservation near the Uinta Range. During the 1980s, leaders from this reservation created more jobs for the Ute. Their most successful businesses include a cattle ranch and a motel and recreational center. The Paiutes and the Gosiutes have smaller reservations elsewhere in the state.

The Navajo Reservation, the largest Indian reservation in the country, extends from Arizona and New Mexico up into southeastern Utah. Nearly half of Utah's Indians live on this reservation.

Many of Utah's Navajo Indians live on a reservation in the southeastern part of the state. Here, a Navajo woman weaves at her home in Monument Valley.

Construction on Salt Lake Temple was completed in 1893. The temple took 40 years to build.

About 70 percent of all Utahns belong to the Church of Jesus Christ of Latter-day Saints. The Salt Lake Temple in Salt Lake City is the world headquarters for the church. Mormons are still expected to donate 10 percent of their income to the church.

Utah has the highest **literacy rate** (a measure of

how many people can read and write) in the nation. Classroom education in Utah began when Mormons set up a school in 1847, shortly after coming to Salt Lake Valley. They pitched a tent that served as a classroom. The first public school opened in 1866.

The Mormon church encourages its members to trace their family roots as far back as possible. The church even has a special library that stores the records people need to chart their family trees. Called the Family History Library, it has one of the world's largest collections of such records.

Reading captures the attention of these Utah students.

Considered one of the top dance companies in the United States, Ballet West performs in Salt Lake City.

   Surrounded by mountains and deserts, Salt Lake City is the largest cultural center for miles around. The Utah Symphony performs in the modern Maurice Abravanel Hall. The Utah Opera Company and Ballet West entertain audiences in the historic Capitol Theatre. Accompanied by a bellowing pipe organ, the 325-member Mormon Tabernacle Choir sings in the Salt Lake Tabernacle, a place of worship. Sports fans attend Utah Jazz basketball games at the Delta Center in Salt Lake City. And Utah's wilderness lends itself to many sporting activities. Its snow-covered mountain slopes attract downhill skiers. Its rivers, pounding against underwater rocks, are ideal for white-water rafting.

Each year thousands of campers, hikers, and horse-back riders tour Utah's canyons. Arches, Bryce Canyon, Canyonlands, Capitol Reef, and Zion are the national parks in Utah, where thousands of acres are set aside as wilderness areas.

Many of the outdoor enthusiasts in Utah are tourists. The state earns about $4 billion each year from visitors. Workers who serve these tourists have service jobs.

About 65 percent of Utah's work-force holds some type of service job. Other Utahns who make a living helping people include doctors, salesclerks, and bank tellers.

In Canyonlands National Park, visitors can camp, hike, and go horseback riding.

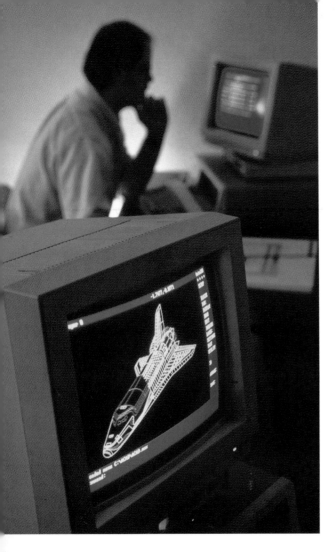

Computer software and spacecraft are developed at Brigham Young University.

Other workers in Utah have jobs working for the government. Most of these jobs are in Salt Lake City, but each city administration also employs workers. In all, 14 percent of the state's workers have government jobs.

Manufacturing employs 11 percent of Utah's workforce. Transportation equipment is the leading manufacturing employer. There are also hundreds of high-tech firms located in the state. Many of these companies develop and manufacture computer parts and software, military equipment, or spacecraft.

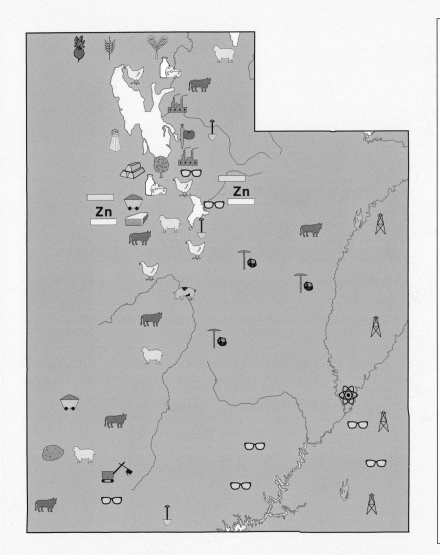

UTAH
Economic Map

The symbols on this map show where different economic activities take place in Utah. The legend below explains what each symbol stands for.

Barley		Oil	
Beef cattle		Potatoes	
Coal		Poultry	
Copper		Salt	
Dairy products		Sand and gravel	
Fruit		Sheep	
Gold		Silver	
Hogs		Sugar beets	
Iron ore		Tourism	
Lead		Uranium	
Manufacturing		Vegetables	
Natural gas		Wheat	

Zn Zinc

Food processing is another leading employer. Foods are canned or frozen at plants in Ogden and Salt Lake City. Dairy products and baked goods are the most important products.

Some people work in factories that smelt (heat and melt) copper ore. Smelting separates the copper from other parts of the ore. Copper ore is mined at Bingham Canyon, one of the world's largest open-pit mines, near Salt Lake City. Other mines in Utah

Copper is mined in Bingham Canyon.

produce coal. About 1 percent of Utah's workers hold jobs in mining.

Utah is a leading supplier of salt. Workers collect tons of crystals from Great Salt Lake every year, using age-old methods of separating the mineral from seawater.

Only 2 percent of Utah's workers make their living as farmers. Of those who do work in agriculture, most raise livestock, mainly beef cattle, turkeys, and sheep. Utah is a leading sheep-raising state, producing more than 3 million pounds of wool a year.

Most crops are grown in the northern part of the state, where water from rivers and mountain streams is used to irrigate fields and orchards. Major crops include wheat, barley, hay, apples, peaches, potatoes, and corn.

Utah has a large population of young people. In the years ahead, Utah will have more young people entering the workforce than other states will. This is one reason why many growing companies are moving to Utah. These firms see Utah's well-educated youth as a key to the future.

In Utah, ranchers and prairie dogs must live side by side.

THE ENVIRONMENT

Saving the Utah Prairie Dog

Like other states, Utah has its share of environmental problems. One problem Utahns are facing is the need to protect wildlife. This need arose long ago, when settlers first tried to earn a living off Utah's land.

The animals of Utah thrived in an unspoiled environment until people began building farms and ranches. At that time, many wild animals had to find new habitats, where they were forced to compete with other animals for food. Some types of animals nearly became extinct.

A Utah prairie dog enjoys a quiet meal.

This prairie dog listens and sniffs to sense danger.

The Utah prairie dog is one example of a species that came close to extinction. From the story of the prairie dog, Utahns know that the loss of a species can affect the environment. They also know that the animals can be saved.

The Utah prairie dog lives only in Utah. Two hundred years ago, the animal's population probably reached well into the millions. In 1900 about 95,000 Utah prairie dogs lived in the state. By 1976 only about 2,100 adult Utah prairie dogs were left.

Prairie dogs use their claws to dig burrows into the soil of wide-open fields.

A Prairie Dog Burrow

A prairie dog designs its burrow with daily needs in mind. The entrance is only a few inches wide—too narrow for large enemies. Near the entrance is a listening post where the prairie dog can listen for enemies. A flood-control room permits the animals to escape drowning during a storm. Another chamber is used as a toilet and is cleaned regularly. A mother keeps her newborns safe and warm in the nursery until they are old enough to go outside the burrow. All burrows have least one emergency exit, which is used when it is not safe to leave through the main entrance.

A prairie dog hardly looks like a poodle or a collie. Instead, this rodent is a relative of the squirrel. Like a squirrel, the prairie dog has a small head and body with short fur. It also has long claws, which it uses for digging, and two large front teeth. The Utah prairie dog has a white tail. Most other types of prairie dogs have black tails.

Utah prairie dogs make their homes in south central Utah, where they find plenty of grasses to eat. They dig underground homes called burrows. Hundreds

Utah prairie dogs stand at the entrance of their burrow.

of burrows in one area make up a prairie dog town.

South central Utah is also home to many livestock farmers. Cattle and sheep graze on the rangelands. When ranchers first started raising livestock in Utah, people looked upon Utah prairie dogs as enemies because they competed with the livestock for grasses to eat.

The grassy land in south central Utah is good for grazing livestock.

In the late 1800s, ranchers complained that their livestock did not have enough food because the prairie dogs were eating most of the grass. And horses, cattle, and sheep occasionally broke a leg when they stepped into the openings of the prairie dogs' burrows.

In Utah and in other states, the ranchers asked the government to help control the number of prairie dogs on farmlands. By the early 1900s, state and U.S. government agencies were spreading poison across prairie dog towns throughout the West. The poison killed much of the prairie dog population. Before long, some people were beginning to wonder if any of the furry little creatures were left.

Widespread poisoning continued until 1963. In 1973 the Utah prairie dog was added to Utah's endangered species list—a listing of specific kinds of wildlife that are close to extinction.

Some of the poison intended for prairie dogs killed other animals as well. Eagles, badgers, and coyotes that ate the poisoned rodents died too. Black-footed ferrets, one of the rarest animals in North America,

In the winter, rattlesnakes live in prairie dog burrows.

were also poisoned. Black-footed ferrets live in burrows along the edges of prairie dog towns.

Other animals also depend on prairie dogs. During the winter, rattlesnakes, insects, and burrowing owls seek shelter from the cold in abandoned prairie dog burrows. In areas where all the prairie dogs had been killed, none were around to dig burrows. The other animals had to leave the area in search of winter homes.

Utahns have worked to help the Utah prairie dog survive.

Since 1973 the government, once in charge of destroying prairie dogs, has been working to increase the rodent's numbers. In Utah, workers use peanut butter or lettuce to capture prairie dogs that burrow on privately owned farmland. The prairie dogs are then released onto Utah's government-owned land, where they will not disturb the ranchers.

The program is working. By 1984 the Utah prairie dog was no longer considered endangered. By 1998 the state had increased the number of prairie dogs to almost 5,000.

Although the rodents are no longer endangered, they are still threatened. A threatened species is one that needs protection to survive. If the transplanted populations of prairie dogs survive and grow on their own, the animal can then be taken off Utah's threatened species list.

Fortunately for Utah prairie dogs, people have learned that changing the environment can hurt wildlife. People also realize that hurting wildlife can change the environment, and Utah prairie dog towns are finding their way back on the map.

ALL ABOUT UTAH

Fun Facts

Utahns named the sea gull their state bird because the insect-eaters saved crops from an invasion of crickets in 1848. The Seagull Monument in Salt Lake City is dedicated to the bird.

The symbol for Paramount Pictures, a major motion-picture company, features Mount Ben Lomond, a mountain peak near Ogden.

In 1991, near Moab, Carl Limone from the College of Eastern Utah Museum uncovered the fossil remains of an unknown dinosaur. The dinosaur was named Utahraptor, which means "Utah's predator."

Sea gulls soar over Great Salt Lake.

One place in Utah allows cars to travel 600 miles per hour! At Bonneville Salt Flats International Speedway, located near Wendover, many car-racing records have been set.

Great Salt Lake, in northern Utah, has been as much as eight times saltier than any of the oceans. Swimmers can float easily in the salt-heavy water.

Utah's nickname, the Beehive State, comes from the state's emblem, a beehive. Mormon settlers named what later became Utah the State of Deseret. Deseret means "honey bee." The beehive was Deseret's emblem as well.

Some Utahns claim that the town of Levan, Utah, got its name because it's located in the center, or navel, of the state. Levan spelled backwards is "navel."

Utah has named the Dutch oven its state cooking pot. The Dutch oven is honored each year at the World Championship Dutch Oven Cookoff, held near Logan, Utah.

STATE SONG

Utah's state song was adopted by the state legislature in 1937. It celebrates the state's mountains, sunny skies, and Utahns' love of their state.

UTAH, WE LOVE THEE

by Evan Stephens

Land of the moun - tains high, U - tah, we love thee!

Land of the sun - ny sky, U - tah, we love thee!

Far in the glo - rious west, Throned on the moun - tain's crest,

In robes of state - hood dressed, U - tah, we love thee!

A UTAH RECIPE

The Navajo are one of many groups of Native Americans who have made their homes in Utah. Fry bread has long been a main food in the Navajo diet. While the recipe may change from region to region, the basic ingredients are the same.

FRY BREAD

You will need:

3 to 5 cups flour
2 tablespoons baking powder
2 teaspoons salt

2 cups water
oil, for frying

1. Fill bottom of a deep skillet with about an inch of oil. Have an adult help you heat oil to 375° F.
2. Combine 2 cups of flour, baking powder, salt, and water. Mix well.
3. Stir in enough of remaining flour to make a soft dough.
4. On a floured surface, knead dough until smooth.
5. Pinch off a 3-inch ball of dough. With your hands, flatten ball and stretch it into a 7-inch circle about ¼-inch thick.
6. Have an adult help you fry the dough in the hot oil. When it turns golden brown, flip it and brown other side.
7. When both sides are brown, remove it from oil. Drain bread on paper towels. Serve with jelly, honey and butter, or soup.

Makes 8–12 servings.

HISTORICAL TIMELINE

10,000 B.C. Groups of Native Americans live throughout Utah.

A.D. 750 Basketmakers begin building pueblos.

1300 Shoshonean-speaking tribes begin settling in the region. Pueblo Indians disappear from Utah.

1776 Francisco Atanasio Domínguez and Silvestre Vélez de Escalante explore Utah.

1800 Fur trappers begin moving through Utah.

1847 Brigham Young and the first Mormon pioneers arrive in Salt Lake Valley.

1848 The United States wins the Utah area from Mexico.

1849 Mormons establish the State of Deseret.

1850 The U.S. Congress creates the Utah Territory.

1853 Ute Indians begin raids on Mormon settlements, sparking the year-long Walker War.

1857 A group of pioneers is attacked by Mormon militiamen. The U.S. government sends troops to the State of Deseret, starting the Utah War.

1861 U.S. troops leave Utah when the Civil War (1861–1865) begins.

1862 U.S. troops arrive in Utah under the command of Patrick Conner, who encourages mining in the area.

1869 At Promontory, Utah, workers finish the nation's first cross-country railroad.

1870s Mining in Utah becomes big business.

1890 Mormon church officials agree to forbid polygamy.

1896 Utah becomes the 45th state to join the Union.

1902 Reed Smoot is elected as the first Mormon U.S. senator.

1959 Missiles are produced and tested on a large scale in Utah.

1986 Construction begins on the Jordanelle Dam.

2002 Salt Lake City hosts the Winter Olympics.

OUTSTANDING UTAHNS

Maurice Abravanel (1903–1993) was the conductor and music director of the Utah Symphony from 1947 to 1979. During his 33 years with the group, Abravanel helped make it one of the leading orchestras in the country.

Maurice Abravanel

Maude Adams (1872–1953), born in Salt Lake City, was a leading actress of the theater. Adams, whose real name was Maude Kiskadden, first appeared on stage at the age of nine months, when she had the title role in *The Lost Child*. She appeared in more than 1,500 performances of *Peter Pan* from 1905 to 1907. Adams starred in many other plays, including *The Little Minister*, *What Every Woman Knows*, and *Quality Street*.

Maude Adams

Roseanne Barr (born 1952) is a comedienne and actress from Salt Lake City. She began her career in 1981, performing in stand-up comedy clubs. From 1988 to 1997, she starred in her own comedy television series called *Roseanne*. From 1998 to 2000, she hosted her own talk show, *The Roseanne Show*.

Roseanne Barr

James P. Beckwourth (1798–1867?) was an African American adventurer of the Wild West. Between 1824 and 1826, Beckwourth trapped animals and dug for gold in Utah. He also explored the region and later wrote about his adventures.

Reva Beck Bosone (1895–1983) is a politician who served in the U.S. House of Representatives from 1949 to 1953. She was the first woman Utahns elected to this office. Beck was born in American Fork, Utah.

Reva Beck Bosone

Jim Bridger (1804–1881), an explorer, was the first white person to discover Great Salt Lake. When he found the salty lake in 1824, he believed he had reached an ocean.

John Moses Browning (1855–1926) was a gunsmith from Ogden who invented the Winchester repeating rifle, the Colt automatic pistol, and the Browning automatic rifle.

Nolan Kay Bushnell

Nolan Kay Bushnell (born 1943), an inventor from Ogden, is considered the father of the video game industry. Bushnell created the first coin-operated video game in 1971 and founded Atari Corporation in 1972. He has founded more than 20 companies, including Chuck E. Cheese.

Jerry Hatten Buss

Jerry Hatten Buss (born 1933) is a real estate executive from Salt Lake City. He owns the Los Angeles Lakers, a professional basketball team.

Butch Cassidy (1866–1909?), a train robber in the days of the Wild West, was also known as Robert LeRoy Parker. The motion picture *Butch Cassidy and the Sundance Kid* is based on Cassidy's life story. Cassidy was born in Beaver, Utah.

Butch Cassidy

Philo Taylor Farnsworth (1906–1971), an inventor, began experimenting with television at the age of 14. At the age of 20, he produced the first all-electronic television image. The electronics whiz gave the first demonstration of television in 1934. Farnsworth was born in Beaver, Utah.

Philo Taylor Farnsworth

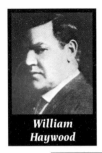

William Haywood

John Marriott

Merlin Olsen

Donny and Marie Osmond

Gene Fullmer (born 1931) is a former boxer who held the title Middleweight Boxing Champion of the World in 1957 and from 1959 to 1962. Fullmer was inducted into the World Boxing Hall of Fame in 1985. He was born in West Jordan, Utah.

William ("Big Bill") Haywood (1869–1928), born in Salt Lake City, was a labor union organizer. He helped establish the Industrial Workers of the World (IWW) in 1905 and became its leader in 1915. Haywood was convicted of antiwar activities during World War I and was sentenced to 20 years in jail. To avoid being imprisoned, he fled to Russia.

John Willard Marriott (1900–1985), a businessman, was born in Marriott, Utah. In 1957 he founded what became one of the country's largest hotel and restaurant chains, the Marriott Corporation.

Merlin Jay Olsen (born 1940), an athlete and actor from Logan, Utah, began his professional football career as a defensive tackle with the Los Angeles Rams. From 1962 to 1973, Olsen was known as one of the Fearsome Foursome. In 1982 he became a member of the Pro Football Hall of Fame. His acting career includes roles in the television series *Little House on the Prairie* and *Father Murphy*.

Donny Osmond (born 1957) and **Marie Osmond** (born 1959) are singers who were born in Ogden. Donny began performing with his brothers at the age of 4, and Marie began her career at the age of 7. The brother and sister starred on the television show *Donny and Marie* from 1976 to 1979. The duo hosted a second *Donny and Marie* show from 1998 to 2000.

Helen Zeese Papanikolas (born 1917) is a writer who has written several books about the settlement of various ethnic groups in Utah. Her novel *The Time of the Little Blackbird* earned the 2000 Utah Book Award for Fiction. Papanikolas, who is of Greek heritage, was born in Carbon County, Utah.

Helen Zeese Papanikolas

Reed Smoot (1862–1941) was the first Mormon to be elected to the U.S. Senate. His membership in the Senate was challenged because he was a high official in a church that had practiced polygamy. In 1907 the Senate ratified his appointment, and he went on to be re-elected four times, serving until 1933. Smoot was born in Salt Lake City.

May Swenson (1919–1989), a poet from Logan, Utah, won several awards for her poetry. Her collections of poems include *A Cage of Spines* and *Half Sun, Half Sleep.*

May Swenson

James Woods (born 1947) is an actor from Vernal. His movie credits include *Salvador, Contact,* and *True Crime.* Woods was the voice of Hades in Disney's animated film *Hercules.*

Brigham Young (1801–1877) led a group of Mormons from Nauvoo, Illinois, to Salt Lake Valley in 1847. The religious leader governed the Utah Territory from 1851 to 1858 and helped to establish a strong Mormon community. He died in Salt Lake City, leaving behind 27 wives and 47 children.

James Woods

Loretta Young (1913–2000) was an actress who appeared in almost 100 motion pictures during the 1930s and 1940s. In 1947 she won an Academy Award for her leading role in *The Farmer's Daughter.* From 1953 to 1963, she hosted her own television show, *The Loretta Young Show.* Young was born in Salt Lake City.

Loretta Young

FACTS-AT-A-GLANCE

Nickname: Beehive State

Song: "Utah, We Love Thee"

Motto: Industry

Flower: sego lily

Tree: blue spruce

Bird: sea gull

Fossil: allosaurus

Fish: Bonneville cutthroat trout

Gem: topaz

Insect: honeybee

Date and ranking of statehood:
    January 4, 1896, the 45th state

Capital: Salt Lake City

Area: 82,168 square miles

Rank in area, nationwide: 12th

Average January temperature: 25° F

Average July temperature: 73° F

Utah's state flag, adopted in 1913, features the state seal. The beehive in the center of the seal stands for industry, or hard work.

POPULATION GROWTH

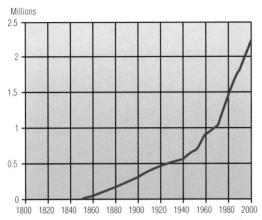

Millions

This chart shows how Utah's population has grown from 1850 to 2000.

Utah's state seal was adopted in 1896. A shield bears the picture of a beehive, the state symbol, and the word "Industry," the state motto. The date 1847 is the year Mormons began settling in Utah. The U.S. flag is on both sides of the shield, and a bald eagle, the U.S. national bird, is perched on top.

Population: 2,233,169 (2000 census)

Rank in population, nationwide: 34th

Major cities and populations: (2000 census) Salt Lake City (181,743), West Valley City (108,896), Provo (105,166), Sandy (88,418), Orem (84,324), Ogden (77,226)

U.S. senators: 2

U.S. representatives: 3

Electoral votes: 5

Natural resources: coal, copper, gold, natural gas, petroleum, salt, sand and gravel, silver, tar sands, uranium

Agricultural products: apples, apricots, barley, beef, cherries, hay, milk, onions, potatoes, wheat, wool

Mining products: coal, copper, gold, natural gas, petroleum, salt, silver

Manufactured goods: chemicals, coal products, computer parts, food products, petroleum products, printed materials, spacecraft, transportation equipment

WHERE UTAHNS WORK

Services—65 percent (services include jobs in trade; community, social, and personal services; finance, insurance, and real estate; transportation, communication, and utilities)

Government—14 percent

Manufacturing—11 percent

Construction—7 percent

Agriculture—2 percent

Mining—1 percent

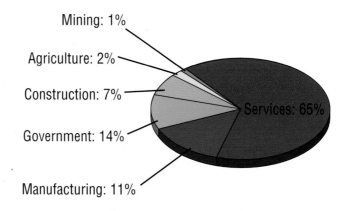

GROSS STATE PRODUCT

Services—62 percent

Government—14 percent

Manufacturing—14 percent

Construction—6 percent

Agriculture—1 percent

Mining—3 percent

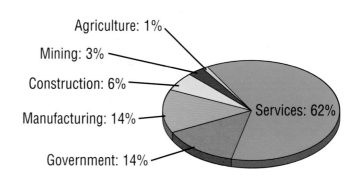

UTAH WILDLIFE

Mammals: American marten, badger, black bear, black-footed ferret, bobcat, lynx, mountain lion, mule deer, Utah prairie dog, wolf

Birds: American goldfinch, bald eagle, black tern, cactus wren, canyon wren, dunlin, grouse, pheasant, spotted sandpiper, whooping crane

Reptiles and amphibians: bullfrog, desert tortoise, Gila monster, plains spadefoot, rattlesnake, red racer, southwestern toad

Fish: bluegill, bonytail chub, grayling, June sucker, perch, razorback sucker, smallmouth bass, Utah chub, Utah sucker, whitefish

Trees: aspen, blue spruce, eastern white pine, juniper, red elder, Rocky Mountain maple, sugar maple, western white pine, white fir

Wild plants: autumn buttercup, cactus, creosote bush, greasewood, mesquite, Navajo sedge, sagebrush, San Rafael cactus, shadscale, toadflax cress

Bald eagle

PLACES TO VISIT

Antelope Island State Park, near Salt Lake City
The largest of the Great Salt Lake's 10 islands, Antelope Island offers many recreational opportunities, such as hiking, sailing, and biking.

Beehive House, Salt Lake City
Visit the official residence of Brigham Young when he was president of the Mormon church and governor of the Utah Territory.

Bonneville Salt Flats
Stretching over 30,000 acres of flat land, the Bonneville Salt Flats draw high-speed auto racers from all over the world.

Canyonlands National Park
Explore mazes of canyons, red rock formations, and prehistoric Native American ruins in Utah's largest national park. View half of the state from the park's observation tower in the Island in the Sky district.

Capitol Reef National Park
A wilderness of sandstone formations and cliffs, Capitol Reef features a variety of deep and narrow twisting canyons. In the Fremont River valley, visitors can see rock art from an ancient Indian culture and the remnants of an early pioneer settlement.

Dinosaur National Monument, near Vernal
    Visitors to the largest quarry of Jurassic period dinosaur
    bones ever discovered can see more than 2,000 dinosaur
    bones exposed in a sandstone wall.

Jensen Historical Farm, Logan
    Step back in time to 1917 at this living history museum.
    Guided tours teach visitors about food preservation, sheep
    shearing, quilting, hay making, threshing, and more.

Museum of Art at Brigham Young University, Provo
    Housed in one of the largest facilities of its kind in the West,
    the museum has a family interactive center, theater, and
    study center.

Museum of Church History and Art, Salt Lake City
    Learn more about the Mormon experience in the 19th and 20th
    centuries through the museum's art and history exhibits.

Temple Square, Salt Lake City
    This 10-acre block is the symbolic heart of the Church of Jesus
    Christ of Latter-day Saints. Twice a week, visitors can hear the
    Salt Lake Mormon Tabernacle Choir at free performances.

ANNUAL EVENTS

St. George Heritage Week—*January*

Bryce Canyon Winter Festival—*February*

Moab Jeep Safari—*April*

Golden Spike Anniversary, Promontory—*May*

Utah Arts Festival, Salt Lake City—*June*

Utah Summer Games, Cedar City—*June*

Ogden Pioneer Days—*July*

Utah Shakespearean Festival, Cedar City—*July-September*

Utah State Fair, Salt Lake City—*September*

Lighting of the Gardens, Vernal—*November*

Temple Square Christmas Lighting, Salt Lake City—*November*

LEARN MORE ABOUT UTAH

BOOKS

General

Fradin, Dennis Brindell. *Utah.* Chicago: Children's Press, 1996.

Kent, Deborah. *Utah.* Danbury, CT: Children's Press, 2000.

Special Interest

Arnold, Caroline. *Dinosaur Mountain: Graveyard of the Past.* New York: Clarion Books, 1989. Read about the discoveries scientists have made at Dinosaur National Monument in Utah.

Hamilton, John. *Butch Cassidy.* Edina, MN: Abdo & Daughters, 1996. This biography describes the life and crimes of Utah's most famous outlaw.

Madsen, Susan Arrington. *I Walked to Zion: True Stories of Young Pioneers on the Mormon Trail.* Salt Lake City, UT: Deseret Books, 1994. Mormons tell how they walked to Utah as children in the 1800s in search of religious freedom.

Marsh, Carole. *A Fun Book of Olympic Trivia: A to Z! Including the 2002 Winter Olympics in Salt Lake City, Utah.* Historic Bath, NC: Gallopade Publishing Group, 2000. This fact-filled book includes information about Utah's capital, host of the 2002 Winter Olympics.

McPherson, Stephanie Sammartino. *TV's Forgotten Hero: The Story of Philo Farnsworth*. Minneapolis: Carolrhoda Books, 1996. This biography of Farnsworth, who invented electronic television, covers the inventor's life from his childhood in Utah to his struggles to recognize his dream.

Fiction

Gregory, Kristiana. *The Great Railroad Race: The Diary of Libby West, Utah Territory, 1868*. New York: Scholastic, 1999. Fourteen-year-old Libby travels through Utah Territory with her family, witnessing the construction of the first transcontinental railroad. Libby fills her diary with the sights and sounds of her travels.

Hulme, Joy N. *Through the Open Door*. New York: HarperCollins, 2000. Nine-year-old Dora and her family are part of a group of Mormons journeying from Utah to New Mexico in 1910.

Litchman, Kristin Embry. *All Is Well*. New York: Delacorte Press, 1998. Set in Salt Lake City in the late 1800s, this story describes the friendship between a young Mormon girl and a non-Mormon girl who moves next door.

Skurzynski, Gloria, and Alane Ferguson. *Ghost Horses*. Washington, D.C.: National Geographic Society, 2000. Set in Utah's Zion National Park, the story follows the adventures of twelve-year-old Jack Landon as he tries to uncover the reasons behind the strange behavior of a band of wild mustangs.

WEBSITES

Welcome to Utah!
<http://www.utah.gov>
The official website for Utah features general information about the state and its government, education system, and more. Visit the kid's page and test your knowledge of Utah trivia.

Utah.com
<http://www.utah.com/>
The official site of the Utah Travel Council lists things to do and places to see in the state.

Salt Lake Tribune
<http://www.sltrib.com>
Utah's largest newspaper provides up-to-date, statewide news and information.

Utah History Encyclopedia
<http://www.media.utah.edu/UHE/UHEindex.html>
This website includes information about and photographs of the people, places, and topics important to Utah history.

Utah Museum of Fine Arts
<http://www.utah.edu/umfa/index.html>
Learn about Utah's only general art museum through its online collections. Follow the link to KidsMuse! for interactive art activities.

PRONUNCIATION GUIDE

Deseret (dehz-uh-REHT)

Gila (HEE-luh)

Gosiute (GOH-shoot)

Nauvoo (naw-VOO)

Navajo (NAV-uh-hoh)

Ouray (oo-RAY)

Paiute (PY-yoot)

polygamy (puh-LIHG-uh-mee)

Shoshone (shuh-SHOHN)

Uinta (yoo-IHN-tuh)

Ute (YOOT)

Acres of farmland stretch across northern Utah.

GLOSSARY

canyon: a narrow valley that has steep rocky cliffs on its sides

desert: an area of land that receives only about 10 inches or less of rain or snow a year

immigrant: a person who moves into a foreign country and settles there

inland sea: a large body of salt water completely surrounded by land and having no outlet

irrigation: watering land by directing water through canals, ditches, pipes, or sprinklers

literacy rate: a measurement of how many people can read and write

plateau: a large, relatively flat area that stands above the surrounding land

polygamy: the practice of one man being married to more than one woman at a time

pueblo: any of the ancient Indian villages in the southwestern United States with buildings of stone or clay, usually built one above the other

reservation: public land set aside by the U.S. government to be used by Native Americans

salt flat: a layer of salt deposits

senator: a member of the U.S. Senate, which is one of the two elected groups that make laws for the United States

tithe: one-tenth of a person's income paid to support a church

tributary: a river or stream that feeds, or flows, into a larger river

INDEX

PHOTO ACKNOWLEDGMENTS

Cover photographs by © David Muench/CORBIS (left) and © Karl Weatherly/COR-BIS (right); PresentationMaps.com, pp. 1, 8, 9, 47; © Richard Cummins/CORBIS, pp. 2–3; © Tom Bean/CORBIS, pp. 3, 52, 58; © Ralph A. Clevinger/CORBIS, pp. 4 (detail), 7 (detail), 17 (detail), 39 (detail), 51 (detail); © Diane Cooper, p. 6; Utah Travel Council, pp. 7, 10, 60; Utah Travel Council/Frank Jensen, pp. 11, 45; Louis and Melvina Hitzeman, p. 12; © David Muench/CORBIS, p. 13; Utah DWR/Jim Weis, p. 14; Utah Department of Natural Resources, pp. 15 (left), 22; © Ron Spomer/Visuals Unlimited, p. 15 (right); Doyen Salsig, pp. 16, 41; Kathleen Marie Menke, p. 17; National Park Service, p. 18; Thomas Henion, pp. 19, 42; Smithsonian Institution National Anthropological Archives, Bureau of American Ethnology Collection, Neg. No. 1633, p. 20; Utah State Historical Society, pp. 21, 23, 26, 29, 30, 33, 35, 36, 66 (top, bottom), 67 (second from bottom, bottom), 69 (top); © Lake County Museum/CORBIS, p. 24; © Church of Jesus Christ of Latter-day Saints, Courtesy of Historical Department, pp. 25, 31; National Cowboy Hall of Fame and Western Heritage Center, p. 28; Union Station Museum, Ogden, Utah, p. 32 (both); © Bettmann/CORBIS, pp. 34, 66 (second from top), 67 (second from top), 68 (second from bottom); © AFP/CORBIS, p. 37; © Ken Redding/CORBIS, p. 38; © Jeff Greenberg@juno.com, p. 39; © Dave G. Houser/CORBIS, p. 40; © Raymond Gehman/CORBIS, p. 43; Salt Lake Convention and Visitors Bureau, p. 44; © Phil Schemeister/CORBIS, p. 46; © Charles E. Rotkin/CORBIS, p. 48; © Scott T. Smith/CORBIS, p. 50; © Jerry L. Ferrara, pp. 51, 54, 55; © Layne Kennedy/CORBIS, p. 53; © Dewitt Jones/CORBIS, p. 57; Jack Lindstrom, p. 61; Tim Seeley, pp. 63, 71, 72; Hollywood Book & Poster Co., p. 66 (second from bottom), 68 (bottom), 69 (bottom); © Roger Ressmeyer/CORBIS, p. 67 (top); Labor History Archives, Wayne State University, p. 68 (top); Marriott Corp., p. 68 (second from top); © Oscar White/CORBIS, p. 69 (second from top); © Henry Diltz/CORBIS, p. 69 (second from bottom); Jean Matheny, p. 70 (top); Laura Westlund, p. 70 (bottom); © Roy Corral/CORBIS, p. 73; Utah Agricultural Experiment Station, p. 80.